This Book Belongs To:

NAME: _____

CONTACT: _____

EMAIL: _____

ADDRESS: _____

_____

INDEX

SOW & BOAR RECORD

PROFILE

NAME: _____   BREED: _____

SEX: _____   COLOR/MARKINGS: _____

DOB: _____   NO. OF TEATS: _____

REG NO.: _____   WEANING DATE/WT: _____

LITTER NO.: _____   ☐ RAISED ☐ PURCHASED

PIG NO.: _____   PURPOSE: _____

PEDIGREE CHART

SIRE: _____

–GRANDSIRE: _____

–GRANDDAM: _____

DAM: _____

–GRANDSIRE: _____

–GRANDDAM: _____

PURCHASE/TRANSFER INFO

_____

_____

_____

NOTES & OTHER DETAILS

PROFILE

NAME: _____   BREED: _____

SEX: _____   COLOR/MARKINGS: _____

DOB: _____   NO. OF TEATS: _____

REG NO.: _____   WEANING DATE/WT: _____

LITTER NO.: _____   ☐ RAISED ☐ PURCHASED

PIG NO.: _____   PURPOSE: _____

PEDIGREE CHART

SIRE: _____

–GRANDSIRE: _____

–GRANDDAM: _____

DAM: _____

–GRANDSIRE: _____

–GRANDDAM: _____

PURCHASE/TRANSFER INFO

_____

_____

_____

NOTES & OTHER DETAILS

PROFILE

NAME: _____   BREED: _____

SEX: _____   COLOR/MARKINGS: _____

DOB: _____   NO. OF TEATS: _____

REG NO.: _____   WEANING DATE/WT: _____

LITTER NO.: _____   ☐ RAISED ☐ PURCHASED

PIG NO.: _____   PURPOSE: _____

PEDIGREE CHART

SIRE: _____

–GRANDSIRE: _____

–GRANDDAM: _____

DAM: _____

–GRANDSIRE: _____

–GRANDDAM: _____

PURCHASE/TRANSFER INFO

_____

_____

NOTES & OTHER DETAILS

SOW & BOAR RECORD

PROFILE

NAME: _____ BREED: _____

SEX: _____ COLOR/MARKINGS: _____

DOB: _____ NO. OF TEATS: _____

REG NO.: _____ WEANING DATE/WT: _____

LITTER NO.: _____ ☐ RAISED ☐ PURCHASED

PIG NO.: _____ PURPOSE: _____

PEDIGREE CHART

SIRE: _____

–GRANDSIRE: _____

–GRANDDAM: _____

DAM: _____

–GRANDSIRE: _____

–GRANDDAM: _____

PURCHASE/TRANSFER INFO

_____

_____

_____

NOTES & OTHER DETAILS

PROFILE

NAME: _____ BREED: _____

SEX: _____ COLOR/MARKINGS: _____

DOB: _____ NO. OF TEATS: _____

REG NO.: _____ WEANING DATE/WT: _____

LITTER NO.: _____ ☐ RAISED ☐ PURCHASED

PIG NO.: _____ PURPOSE: _____

PEDIGREE CHART

SIRE: _____

–GRANDSIRE: _____

–GRANDDAM: _____

DAM: _____

–GRANDSIRE: _____

–GRANDDAM: _____

PURCHASE/TRANSFER INFO

_____

_____

_____

NOTES & OTHER DETAILS

PROFILE

NAME: _____ BREED: _____

SEX: _____ COLOR/MARKINGS: _____

DOB: _____ NO. OF TEATS: _____

REG NO.: _____ WEANING DATE/WT: _____

LITTER NO.: _____ ☐ RAISED ☐ PURCHASED

PIG NO.: _____ PURPOSE: _____

PEDIGREE CHART

SIRE: _____

–GRANDSIRE: _____

–GRANDDAM: _____

DAM: _____

–GRANDSIRE: _____

–GRANDDAM: _____

PURCHASE/TRANSFER INFO

_____

_____

_____

NOTES & OTHER DETAILS

SOW & BOAR RECORD

PROFILE

NAME: _____ BREED: _____

SEX: _____ COLOR/MARKINGS: _____

DOB: _____ NO. OF TEATS: _____

REG NO.: _____ WEANING DATE/WT: _____

LITTER NO.: _____ RAISED   PURCHASED

PIG NO.: _____ PURPOSE: _____

PEDIGREE CHART

SIRE: _____

–GRANDSIRE: _____

–GRANDDAM: _____

DAM: _____

–GRANDSIRE: _____

–GRANDDAM: _____

PURCHASE/TRANSFER INFO

_____

_____

_____

NOTES & OTHER DETAILS

PROFILE

NAME: _____ BREED: _____

SEX: _____ COLOR/MARKINGS: _____

DOB: _____ NO. OF TEATS: _____

REG NO.: _____ WEANING DATE/WT: _____

LITTER NO.: _____ RAISED   PURCHASED

PIG NO.: _____ PURPOSE: _____

PEDIGREE CHART

SIRE: _____

–GRANDSIRE: _____

–GRANDDAM: _____

DAM: _____

–GRANDSIRE: _____

–GRANDDAM: _____

PURCHASE/TRANSFER INFO

_____

_____

_____

NOTES & OTHER DETAILS

PROFILE

NAME: _____ BREED: _____

SEX: _____ COLOR/MARKINGS: _____

DOB: _____ NO. OF TEATS: _____

REG NO.: _____ WEANING DATE/WT: _____

LITTER NO.: _____ RAISED   PURCHASED

PIG NO.: _____ PURPOSE: _____

PEDIGREE CHART

SIRE: _____

–GRANDSIRE: _____

–GRANDDAM: _____

DAM: _____

–GRANDSIRE: _____

–GRANDDAM: _____

PURCHASE/TRANSFER INFO

_____

_____

NOTES & OTHER DETAILS

SOW & BOAR RECORD

PROFILE

NAME: _____ BREED: _____

SEX: _____ COLOR/MARKINGS: _____

DOB: _____ NO. OF TEATS: _____

REG NO.: _____ WEANING DATE/WT: _____

LITTER NO.: _____ ☐ RAISED ☐ PURCHASED

PIG NO.: _____ PURPOSE: _____

PEDIGREE CHART

SIRE: _____

–GRANDSIRE: _____

–GRANDDAM: _____

DAM: _____

–GRANDSIRE: _____

–GRANDDAM: _____

PURCHASE/TRANSFER INFO

_____
_____
_____

NOTES & OTHER DETAILS

PROFILE

NAME: _____ BREED: _____

SEX: _____ COLOR/MARKINGS: _____

DOB: _____ NO. OF TEATS: _____

REG NO.: _____ WEANING DATE/WT: _____

LITTER NO.: _____ ☐ RAISED ☐ PURCHASED

PIG NO.: _____ PURPOSE: _____

PEDIGREE CHART

SIRE: _____

–GRANDSIRE: _____

–GRANDDAM: _____

DAM: _____

–GRANDSIRE: _____

–GRANDDAM: _____

PURCHASE/TRANSFER INFO

_____
_____
_____

NOTES & OTHER DETAILS

PROFILE

NAME: _____ BREED: _____

SEX: _____ COLOR/MARKINGS: _____

DOB: _____ NO. OF TEATS: _____

REG NO.: _____ WEANING DATE/WT: _____

LITTER NO.: _____ ☐ RAISED ☐ PURCHASED

PIG NO.: _____ PURPOSE: _____

PEDIGREE CHART

SIRE: _____

–GRANDSIRE: _____

–GRANDDAM: _____

DAM: _____

–GRANDSIRE: _____

–GRANDDAM: _____

PURCHASE/TRANSFER INFO

_____
_____
_____

NOTES & OTHER DETAILS

SOW & BOAR RECORD

PROFILE

NAME: _____ BREED: _____

SEX: _____ COLOR/MARKINGS: _____

DOB: _____ NO. OF TEATS: _____

REG NO.: _____ WEANING DATE/WT: _____

LITTER NO.: _____ ☐ RAISED ☐ PURCHASED

PIG NO.: _____ PURPOSE: _____

PEDIGREE CHART

SIRE: _____

–GRANDSIRE: _____

–GRANDDAM: _____

DAM: _____

–GRANDSIRE: _____

–GRANDDAM: _____

PURCHASE/TRANSFER INFO

_____
_____
_____

NOTES & OTHER DETAILS

PROFILE

NAME: _____ BREED: _____

SEX: _____ COLOR/MARKINGS: _____

DOB: _____ NO. OF TEATS: _____

REG NO.: _____ WEANING DATE/WT: _____

LITTER NO.: _____ ☐ RAISED ☐ PURCHASED

PIG NO.: _____ PURPOSE: _____

PEDIGREE CHART

SIRE: _____

–GRANDSIRE: _____

–GRANDDAM: _____

DAM: _____

–GRANDSIRE: _____

–GRANDDAM: _____

PURCHASE/TRANSFER INFO

_____
_____
_____

NOTES & OTHER DETAILS

PROFILE

NAME: _____ BREED: _____

SEX: _____ COLOR/MARKINGS: _____

DOB: _____ NO. OF TEATS: _____

REG NO.: _____ WEANING DATE/WT: _____

LITTER NO.: _____ ☐ RAISED ☐ PURCHASED

PIG NO.: _____ PURPOSE: _____

PEDIGREE CHART

SIRE: _____

–GRANDSIRE: _____

–GRANDDAM: _____

DAM: _____

–GRANDSIRE: _____

–GRANDDAM: _____

PURCHASE/TRANSFER INFO

_____
_____
_____

NOTES & OTHER DETAILS

SOW & BOAR RECORD

PROFILE

NAME: _____ BREED: _____

SEX: _____ COLOR/MARKINGS: _____

DOB: _____ NO. OF TEATS: _____

REG NO.: _____ WEANING DATE/WT: _____

LITTER NO.: _____ ☐ RAISED ☐ PURCHASED

PIG NO.: _____ PURPOSE: _____

PEDIGREE CHART

SIRE: _____

–GRANDSIRE: _____

–GRANDDAM: _____

DAM: _____

–GRANDSIRE: _____

–GRANDDAM: _____

PURCHASE/TRANSFER INFO

_____

_____

_____

NOTES & OTHER DETAILS

PROFILE

NAME: _____ BREED: _____

SEX: _____ COLOR/MARKINGS: _____

DOB: _____ NO. OF TEATS: _____

REG NO.: _____ WEANING DATE/WT: _____

LITTER NO.: _____ ☐ RAISED ☐ PURCHASED

PIG NO.: _____ PURPOSE: _____

PEDIGREE CHART

SIRE: _____

–GRANDSIRE: _____

–GRANDDAM: _____

DAM: _____

–GRANDSIRE: _____

–GRANDDAM: _____

PURCHASE/TRANSFER INFO

_____

_____

_____

NOTES & OTHER DETAILS

PROFILE

NAME: _____ BREED: _____

SEX: _____ COLOR/MARKINGS: _____

DOB: _____ NO. OF TEATS: _____

REG NO.: _____ WEANING DATE/WT: _____

LITTER NO.: _____ ☐ RAISED ☐ PURCHASED

PIG NO.: _____ PURPOSE: _____

PEDIGREE CHART

SIRE: _____

–GRANDSIRE: _____

–GRANDDAM: _____

DAM: _____

–GRANDSIRE: _____

–GRANDDAM: _____

PURCHASE/TRANSFER INFO

_____

_____

_____

NOTES & OTHER DETAILS

SOW & BOAR RECORD

PROFILE

NAME: _____ BREED: _____

SEX: _____ COLOR/MARKINGS: _____

DOB: _____ NO. OF TEATS: _____

REG NO.: _____ WEANING DATE/WT: _____

LITTER NO.: _____ ☐ RAISED ☐ PURCHASED

PIG NO.: _____ PURPOSE: _____

PEDIGREE CHART

SIRE: _____

–GRANDSIRE: _____

–GRANDDAM: _____

DAM: _____

–GRANDSIRE: _____

–GRANDDAM: _____

PURCHASE/TRANSFER INFO

_____

_____

_____

NOTES & OTHER DETAILS

PROFILE

NAME: _____ BREED: _____

SEX: _____ COLOR/MARKINGS: _____

DOB: _____ NO. OF TEATS: _____

REG NO.: _____ WEANING DATE/WT: _____

LITTER NO.: _____ ☐ RAISED ☐ PURCHASED

PIG NO.: _____ PURPOSE: _____

PEDIGREE CHART

SIRE: _____

–GRANDSIRE: _____

–GRANDDAM: _____

DAM: _____

–GRANDSIRE: _____

–GRANDDAM: _____

PURCHASE/TRANSFER INFO

_____

_____

_____

NOTES & OTHER DETAILS

PROFILE

NAME: _____ BREED: _____

SEX: _____ COLOR/MARKINGS: _____

DOB: _____ NO. OF TEATS: _____

REG NO.: _____ WEANING DATE/WT: _____

LITTER NO.: _____ ☐ RAISED ☐ PURCHASED

PIG NO.: _____ PURPOSE: _____

PEDIGREE CHART

SIRE: _____

–GRANDSIRE: _____

–GRANDDAM: _____

DAM: _____

–GRANDSIRE: _____

–GRANDDAM: _____

PURCHASE/TRANSFER INFO

_____

_____

NOTES & OTHER DETAILS

SOW & BOAR RECORD

PROFILE

NAME: _____ BREED: _____

SEX: _____ COLOR/MARKINGS: _____

DOB: _____ NO. OF TEATS: _____

REG NO.: _____ WEANING DATE/WT: _____

LITTER NO.: _____ ☐ RAISED ☐ PURCHASED

PIG NO.: _____ PURPOSE: _____

PEDIGREE CHART

SIRE: _____

–GRANDSIRE: _____

–GRANDDAM: _____

DAM: _____

–GRANDSIRE: _____

–GRANDDAM: _____

PURCHASE/TRANSFER INFO

_____

_____

_____

NOTES & OTHER DETAILS

PROFILE

NAME: _____ BREED: _____

SEX: _____ COLOR/MARKINGS: _____

DOB: _____ NO. OF TEATS: _____

REG NO.: _____ WEANING DATE/WT: _____

LITTER NO.: _____ ☐ RAISED ☐ PURCHASED

PIG NO.: _____ PURPOSE: _____

PEDIGREE CHART

SIRE: _____

–GRANDSIRE: _____

–GRANDDAM: _____

DAM: _____

–GRANDSIRE: _____

–GRANDDAM: _____

PURCHASE/TRANSFER INFO

_____

_____

_____

NOTES & OTHER DETAILS

PROFILE

NAME: _____ BREED: _____

SEX: _____ COLOR/MARKINGS: _____

DOB: _____ NO. OF TEATS: _____

REG NO.: _____ WEANING DATE/WT: _____

LITTER NO.: _____ ☐ RAISED ☐ PURCHASED

PIG NO.: _____ PURPOSE: _____

PEDIGREE CHART

SIRE: _____

–GRANDSIRE: _____

–GRANDDAM: _____

DAM: _____

–GRANDSIRE: _____

–GRANDDAM: _____

PURCHASE/TRANSFER INFO

_____

_____

_____

NOTES & OTHER DETAILS

SOW & BOAR RECORD

PROFILE

NAME: _____ BREED: _____

SEX: _____ COLOR/MARKINGS: _____

DOB: _____ NO. OF TEATS: _____

REG NO.: _____ WEANING DATE/WT: _____

LITTER NO.: _____ ☐ RAISED ☐ PURCHASED

PIG NO.: _____ PURPOSE: _____

PEDIGREE CHART

SIRE: _____

–GRANDSIRE: _____

–GRANDDAM: _____

DAM: _____

–GRANDSIRE: _____

–GRANDDAM: _____

PURCHASE/TRANSFER INFO

_____
_____
_____

NOTES & OTHER DETAILS

PROFILE

NAME: _____ BREED: _____

SEX: _____ COLOR/MARKINGS: _____

DOB: _____ NO. OF TEATS: _____

REG NO.: _____ WEANING DATE/WT: _____

LITTER NO.: _____ ☐ RAISED ☐ PURCHASED

PIG NO.: _____ PURPOSE: _____

PEDIGREE CHART

SIRE: _____

–GRANDSIRE: _____

–GRANDDAM: _____

DAM: _____

–GRANDSIRE: _____

–GRANDDAM: _____

PURCHASE/TRANSFER INFO

_____
_____
_____

NOTES & OTHER DETAILS

PROFILE

NAME: _____ BREED: _____

SEX: _____ COLOR/MARKINGS: _____

DOB: _____ NO. OF TEATS: _____

REG NO.: _____ WEANING DATE/WT: _____

LITTER NO.: _____ ☐ RAISED ☐ PURCHASED

PIG NO.: _____ PURPOSE: _____

PEDIGREE CHART

SIRE: _____

–GRANDSIRE: _____

–GRANDDAM: _____

DAM: _____

–GRANDSIRE: _____

–GRANDDAM: _____

PURCHASE/TRANSFER INFO

_____
_____
_____

NOTES & OTHER DETAILS

SOW & BOAR RECORD

PROFILE

NAME: _____ BREED: _____

SEX: _____ COLOR/MARKINGS: _____

DOB: _____ NO. OF TEATS: _____

REG NO.: _____ WEANING DATE/WT: _____

LITTER NO.: _____ ☐ RAISED ☐ PURCHASED

PIG NO.: _____ PURPOSE: _____

PEDIGREE CHART

SIRE: _____

–GRANDSIRE: _____

–GRANDDAM: _____

DAM: _____

–GRANDSIRE: _____

–GRANDDAM: _____

PURCHASE/TRANSFER INFO

_____
_____
_____

NOTES & OTHER DETAILS

PROFILE

NAME: _____ BREED: _____

SEX: _____ COLOR/MARKINGS: _____

DOB: _____ NO. OF TEATS: _____

REG NO.: _____ WEANING DATE/WT: _____

LITTER NO.: _____ ☐ RAISED ☐ PURCHASED

PIG NO.: _____ PURPOSE: _____

PEDIGREE CHART

SIRE: _____

–GRANDSIRE: _____

–GRANDDAM: _____

DAM: _____

–GRANDSIRE: _____

–GRANDDAM: _____

PURCHASE/TRANSFER INFO

_____
_____
_____

NOTES & OTHER DETAILS

PROFILE

NAME: _____ BREED: _____

SEX: _____ COLOR/MARKINGS: _____

DOB: _____ NO. OF TEATS: _____

REG NO.: _____ WEANING DATE/WT: _____

LITTER NO.: _____ ☐ RAISED ☐ PURCHASED

PIG NO.: _____ PURPOSE: _____

PEDIGREE CHART

SIRE: _____

–GRANDSIRE: _____

–GRANDDAM: _____

DAM: _____

–GRANDSIRE: _____

–GRANDDAM: _____

PURCHASE/TRANSFER INFO

_____
_____
_____

NOTES & OTHER DETAILS

SOW & BOAR RECORD

PROFILE

NAME: BREED:

SEX: COLOR/MARKINGS:

DOB: NO. OF TEATS:

REG NO.:   WEANING DATE/WT:

LITTER NO.:   RAISED   PURCHASED

PIG NO.:   PURPOSE:

PEDIGREE CHART

SIRE:

–GRANDSIRE:

–GRANDDAM:

DAM:

–GRANDSIRE:

–GRANDDAM:

PURCHASE/TRANSFER INFO

NOTES & OTHER DETAILS

PROFILE

NAME: BREED:

SEX: COLOR/MARKINGS:

DOB: NO. OF TEATS:

REG NO.:   WEANING DATE/WT:

LITTER NO.:   RAISED   PURCHASED

PIG NO.:   PURPOSE:

PEDIGREE CHART

SIRE:

–GRANDSIRE:

–GRANDDAM:

DAM:

–GRANDSIRE:

–GRANDDAM:

PURCHASE/TRANSFER INFO

NOTES & OTHER DETAILS

PROFILE

NAME: BREED:

SEX: COLOR/MARKINGS:

DOB: NO. OF TEATS:

REG NO.:   WEANING DATE/WT:

LITTER NO.:   RAISED   PURCHASED

PIG NO.:   PURPOSE:

PEDIGREE CHART

SIRE:

–GRANDSIRE:

–GRANDDAM:

DAM:

–GRANDSIRE:

–GRANDDAM:

PURCHASE/TRANSFER INFO

NOTES & OTHER DETAILS

SOW & BOAR RECORD

PROFILE

NAME: _____ BREED: _____

SEX: _____ COLOR/MARKINGS: _____

DOB: _____ NO. OF TEATS: _____

REG NO.: _____ WEANING DATE/WT: _____

LITTER NO.: _____ ☐ RAISED ☐ PURCHASED

PIG NO.: _____ PURPOSE: _____

PEDIGREE CHART

SIRE: _____

–GRANDSIRE: _____

–GRANDDAM: _____

DAM: _____

–GRANDSIRE: _____

–GRANDDAM: _____

PURCHASE/TRANSFER INFO

_____

_____

_____

NOTES & OTHER DETAILS

PROFILE

NAME: _____ BREED: _____

SEX: _____ COLOR/MARKINGS: _____

DOB: _____ NO. OF TEATS: _____

REG NO.: _____ WEANING DATE/WT: _____

LITTER NO.: _____ ☐ RAISED ☐ PURCHASED

PIG NO.: _____ PURPOSE: _____

PEDIGREE CHART

SIRE: _____

–GRANDSIRE: _____

–GRANDDAM: _____

DAM: _____

–GRANDSIRE: _____

–GRANDDAM: _____

PURCHASE/TRANSFER INFO

_____

_____

_____

NOTES & OTHER DETAILS

PROFILE

NAME: _____ BREED: _____

SEX: _____ COLOR/MARKINGS: _____

DOB: _____ NO. OF TEATS: _____

REG NO.: _____ WEANING DATE/WT: _____

LITTER NO.: _____ ☐ RAISED ☐ PURCHASED

PIG NO.: _____ PURPOSE: _____

PEDIGREE CHART

SIRE: _____

–GRANDSIRE: _____

–GRANDDAM: _____

DAM: _____

–GRANDSIRE: _____

–GRANDDAM: _____

PURCHASE/TRANSFER INFO

_____

_____

_____

NOTES & OTHER DETAILS

BREEDING RECORD

BOAR ID, DOB	SOW ID, DOB	SOW ESTRUS DATE, DURATION	SERVICE DATES	EST. FARROWING DATE	NOTES

FARROWING RECORD

DAM & AGE	SIRE	FARROW-ING DATE	LIT-TER #	# BORN ALIVE, M/F	# BORN DEAD, M/F	AVG BW	WEANING			NOTES
							DATE	# OF PIGS	AVG WT	

BREEDING RECORD

BOAR ID, DOB	SOW ID, DOB	SOW ESTRUS DATE, DURATION	SERVICE DATES	EST. FARROW- ING DATE	NOTES

FARROWING RECORD

DAM & AGE	SIRE	FARROW-ING DATE	LIT-TER #	# BORN ALIVE, M/F	# BORN DEAD, M/F	AVG BW	WEANING			NOTES
							DATE	# OF PIGS	AVG WT	

BREEDING RECORD

BOAR ID, DOB	SOW ID, DOB	SOW ESTRUS DATE, DURATION	SERVICE DATES	EST. FARROW-ING DATE	NOTES

FARROWING RECORD

DAM & AGE	SIRE	FARROW-ING DATE	LIT-TER #	# BORN ALIVE, M/F	# BORN DEAD, M/F	AVG BW	WEANING			NOTES
							DATE	# OF PIGS	AVG WT	

BREEDING RECORD

BOAR ID, DOB	SOW ID, DOB	SOW ESTRUS DATE, DURATION	SERVICE DATES	EST. FARROW- ING DATE	NOTES

FARROWING RECORD

DAM & AGE	SIRE	FARROW-ING DATE	LIT-TER #	# BORN ALIVE, M/F	# BORN DEAD, M/F	AVG BW	WEANING			NOTES
							DATE	# OF PIGS	AVG WT	

BREEDING RECORD

BOAR ID, DOB	SOW ID, DOB	SOW ESTRUS DATE, DURATION	SERVICE DATES	EST. FARROW-ING DATE	NOTES

FARROWING RECORD

DAM & AGE	SIRE	FARROW-ING DATE	LIT-TER #	# BORN ALIVE, M/F	# BORN DEAD, M/F	AVG BW	WEANING			NOTES
							DATE	# OF PIGS	AVG WT	

BREEDING RECORD

BOAR ID, DOB	SOW ID, DOB	SOW ESTRUS DATE, DURATION	SERVICE DATES	EST. FARROW-ING DATE	NOTES

FARROWING RECORD

DAM & AGE	SIRE	FARROW- ING DATE	LIT- TER #	# BORN ALIVE, M/F	# BORN DEAD, M/F	AVG BW	WEANING			NOTES
							DATE	# OF PIGS	AVG WT	

BREEDING RECORD

BOAR ID, DOB	SOW ID, DOB	SOW ESTRUS DATE, DURATION	SERVICE DATES	EST. FARROW-ING DATE	NOTES

FARROWING RECORD

DAM & AGE	SIRE	FARROW-ING DATE	LIT-TER #	# BORN ALIVE, M/F	# BORN DEAD, M/F	AVG BW	WEANING			NOTES
							DATE	# OF PIGS	AVG WT	

BREEDING RECORD

BOAR ID, DOB	SOW ID, DOB	SOW ESTRUS DATE, DURATION	SERVICE DATES	EST. FARROW-ING DATE	NOTES

FARROWING RECORD

DAM & AGE	SIRE	FARROW-ING DATE	LIT-TER #	# BORN ALIVE, M/F	# BORN DEAD, M/F	AVG BW	WEANING			NOTES
							DATE	# OF PIGS	AVG WT	

BREEDING RECORD

BOAR ID, DOB	SOW ID, DOB	SOW ESTRUS DATE, DURATION	SERVICE DATES	EST. FARROW-ING DATE	NOTES

FARROWING RECORD

DAM & AGE	SIRE	FARROW- ING DATE	LIT- TER #	# BORN ALIVE, M/F	# BORN DEAD, M/F	AVG BW	WEANING			NOTES
							DATE	# OF PIGS	AVG WT	

BREEDING RECORD

BOAR ID, DOB	SOW ID, DOB	SOW ESTRUS DATE, DURATION	SERVICE DATES	EST. FARROW-ING DATE	NOTES

FARROWING RECORD

DAM & AGE	SIRE	FARROW-ING DATE	LIT-TER #	# BORN ALIVE, M/F	# BORN DEAD, M/F	AVG BW	WEANING			NOTES
							DATE	# OF PIGS	AVG WT	

BREEDING RECORD

BOAR ID, DOB	SOW ID, DOB	SOW ESTRUS DATE, DURATION	SERVICE DATES	EST. FARROW- ING DATE	NOTES

FARROWING RECORD

DAM & AGE	SIRE	FARROW-ING DATE	LIT-TER #	# BORN ALIVE, M/F	# BORN DEAD, M/F	AVG BW	WEANING			NOTES
							DATE	# OF PIGS	AVG WT	

BREEDING RECORD

BOAR ID, DOB	SOW ID, DOB	SOW ESTRUS DATE, DURATION	SERVICE DATES	EST. FARROW-ING DATE	NOTES

FARROWING RECORD

DAM & AGE	SIRE	FARROW-ING DATE	LIT-TER #	# BORN ALIVE, M/F	# BORN DEAD, M/F	AVG BW	WEANING			NOTES
							DATE	# OF PIGS	AVG WT	

BREEDING RECORD

BOAR ID, DOB	SOW ID, DOB	SOW ESTRUS DATE, DURATION	SERVICE DATES	EST. FARROW- ING DATE	NOTES

FARROWING RECORD

DAM & AGE	SIRE	FARROW-ING DATE	LIT-TER #	# BORN ALIVE, M/F	# BORN DEAD, M/F	AVG BW	WEANING			NOTES
							DATE	# OF PIGS	AVG WT	

BREEDING RECORD

BOAR ID, DOB	SOW ID, DOB	SOW ESTRUS DATE, DURATION	SERVICE DATES	EST. FARROW-ING DATE	NOTES

FARROWING RECORD

DAM & AGE	SIRE	FARROW-ING DATE	LIT-TER #	# BORN ALIVE, M/F	# BORN DEAD, M/F	AVG BW	WEANING			NOTES
							DATE	# OF PIGS	AVG WT	

BREEDING RECORD

BOAR ID, DOB	SOW ID, DOB	SOW ESTRUS DATE, DURATION	SERVICE DATES	EST. FARROW- ING DATE	NOTES

FARROWING RECORD

DAM & AGE	SIRE	FARROW-ING DATE	LIT-TER #	# BORN ALIVE, M/F	# BORN DEAD, M/F	AVG BW	WEANING			NOTES
							DATE	# OF PIGS	AVG WT	

BREEDING RECORD

BOAR ID, DOB	SOW ID, DOB	SOW ESTRUS DATE, DURATION	SERVICE DATES	EST. FARROW- ING DATE	NOTES

FARROWING RECORD

DAM & AGE	SIRE	FARROW-ING DATE	LIT-TER #	# BORN ALIVE, M/F	# BORN DEAD, M/F	AVG BW	WEANING			NOTES
							DATE	# OF PIGS	AVG WT	

LITTER RECORD

SOURCE/ LITTER NO.	PIG'S NO.	M/F	DOB, BW	DEFECTS & ABNORMALITIES	WEANING DATE & WT	CASTRA- TION DATE	DATE OF DEATH, CAUSE	NOTES

LITTER RECORD

SOURCE/ LITTER NO.	PIG'S NO.	M/F	DOB, BW	DEFECTS & ABNORMALITIES	WEANING DATE & WT	CASTRA- TION DATE	DATE OF DEATH, CAUSE	NOTES

LITTER RECORD

SOURCE/ LITTER NO.	PIG'S NO.	M/F	DOB, BW	DEFECTS & ABNORMALITIES	WEANING DATE & WT	CASTRA- TION DATE	DATE OF DEATH, CAUSE	NOTES

LITTER RECORD

SOURCE/ LITTER NO.	PIG'S NO.	M/F	DOB, BW	DEFECTS & ABNORMALITIES	WEANING DATE & WT	CASTRA- TION DATE	DATE OF DEATH, CAUSE	NOTES

LITTER RECORD

SOURCE/ LITTER NO.	PIG'S NO.	M/F	DOB, BW	DEFECTS & ABNORMALITIES	WEANING DATE & WT	CASTRA- TION DATE	DATE OF DEATH, CAUSE	NOTES

LITTER RECORD

SOURCE/ LITTER NO.	PIG'S NO.	M/F	DOB, BW	DEFECTS & ABNORMALITIES	WEANING DATE & WT	CASTRA- TION DATE	DATE OF DEATH, CAUSE	NOTES

LITTER RECORD

SOURCE/ LITTER NO.	PIG'S NO.	M/F	DOB, BW	DEFECTS & ABNORMALITIES	WEANING DATE & WT	CASTRA-TION DATE	DATE OF DEATH, CAUSE	NOTES

LITTER RECORD

SOURCE/ LITTER NO.	PIG'S NO.	M/F	DOB, BW	DEFECTS & ABNORMALITIES	WEANING DATE & WT	CASTRA- TION DATE	DATE OF DEATH, CAUSE	NOTES

LITTER RECORD

SOURCE/ LITTER NO.	PIG'S NO.	M/F	DOB, BW	DEFECTS & ABNORMALITIES	WEANING DATE & WT	CASTRA- TION DATE	DATE OF DEATH, CAUSE	NOTES

LITTER RECORD

SOURCE/ LITTER NO.	PIG'S NO.	M/F	DOB, BW	DEFECTS & ABNORMALITIES	WEANING DATE & WT	CASTRA- TION DATE	DATE OF DEATH, CAUSE	NOTES

LITTER RECORD

SOURCE/ LITTER NO.	PIG'S NO.	M/F	DOB, BW	DEFECTS & ABNORMALITIES	WEANING DATE & WT	CASTRA- TION DATE	DATE OF DEATH, CAUSE	NOTES

LITTER RECORD

SOURCE/ LITTER NO.	PIG'S NO.	M/F	DOB, BW	DEFECTS & ABNORMALITIES	WEANING DATE & WT	CASTRA- TION DATE	DATE OF DEATH, CAUSE	NOTES

LITTER RECORD

SOURCE/ LITTER NO.	PIG'S NO.	M/F	DOB, BW	DEFECTS & ABNORMALITIES	WEANING DATE & WT	CASTRA- TION DATE	DATE OF DEATH, CAUSE	NOTES

LITTER RECORD

SOURCE/ LITTER NO.	PIG'S NO.	M/F	DOB, BW	DEFECTS & ABNORMALITIES	WEANING DATE & WT	CASTRA- TION DATE	DATE OF DEATH, CAUSE	NOTES

LITTER RECORD

SOURCE/ LITTER NO.	PIG'S NO.	M/F	DOB, BW	DEFECTS & ABNORMALITIES	WEANING DATE & WT	CASTRA- TION DATE	DATE OF DEATH, CAUSE	NOTES

LITTER RECORD

SOURCE/ LITTER NO.	PIG'S NO.	M/F	DOB, BW	DEFECTS & ABNORMALITIES	WEANING DATE & WT	CASTRA- TION DATE	DATE OF DEATH, CAUSE	NOTES

LITTER RECORD

SOURCE/ LITTER NO.	PIG'S NO.	M/F	DOB, BW	DEFECTS & ABNORMALITIES	WEANING DATE & WT	CASTRA- TION DATE	DATE OF DEATH, CAUSE	NOTES

LITTER RECORD

SOURCE/ LITTER NO.	PIG'S NO.	M/F	DOB, BW	DEFECTS & ABNORMALITIES	WEANING DATE & WT	CASTRA- TION DATE	DATE OF DEATH, CAUSE	NOTES

DEWORMING & IMMUNIZATIONS

DATE	LITTER/ID	VACCINE/TX	COMPANY	DOSAGE	DUE NEXT	NOTES

DEWORMING & IMMUNIZATIONS

DATE	LITTER/ID	VACCINE/TX	COMPANY	DOSAGE	DUE NEXT	NOTES

DEWORMING & IMMUNIZATIONS

DATE	LITTER/ID	VACCINE/TX	COMPANY	DOSAGE	DUE NEXT	NOTES

DEWORMING & IMMUNIZATIONS

DATE	LITTER/ID	VACCINE/TX	COMPANY	DOSAGE	DUE NEXT	NOTES

DEWORMING & IMMUNIZATIONS

DATE	LITTER/ID	VACCINE/TX	COMPANY	DOSAGE	DUE NEXT	NOTES

DEWORMING & IMMUNIZATIONS

DATE	LITTER/ID	VACCINE/TX	COMPANY	DOSAGE	DUE NEXT	NOTES

DEWORMING & IMMUNIZATIONS

DATE	LITTER/ID	VACCINE/TX	COMPANY	DOSAGE	DUE NEXT	NOTES

DEWORMING & IMMUNIZATIONS

DATE	LITTER/ID	VACCINE/TX	COMPANY	DOSAGE	DUE NEXT	NOTES

DEWORMING & IMMUNIZATIONS

DATE	LITTER/ID	VACCINE/TX	COMPANY	DOSAGE	DUE NEXT	NOTES

DEWORMING & IMMUNIZATIONS

DATE	LITTER/ID	VACCINE/TX	COMPANY	DOSAGE	DUE NEXT	NOTES

MEDICAL TREATMENT

NAME/ ID	DATE/ PERIOD	DX/ CONDITION	TREATMENT/TEST/ PROCEDURE	DOSAGE	COST	NOTES

MEDICAL TREATMENT

NAME/ ID	DATE/ PERIOD	DX/ CONDITION	TREATMENT/TEST/ PROCEDURE	DOSAGE	COST	NOTES

MEDICAL TREATMENT

NAME/ ID	DATE/ PERIOD	DX/ CONDITION	TREATMENT/TEST/ PROCEDURE	DOSAGE	COST	NOTES

MEDICAL TREATMENT

NAME/ ID	DATE/ PERIOD	DX/ CONDITION	TREATMENT/TEST/ PROCEDURE	DOSAGE	COST	NOTES

MEDICAL TREATMENT

NAME/ ID	DATE/ PERIOD	DX/ CONDITION	TREATMENT/TEST/ PROCEDURE	DOSAGE	COST	NOTES

MEDICAL TREATMENT

NAME/ ID	DATE/ PERIOD	DX/ CONDITION	TREATMENT/TEST/ PROCEDURE	DOSAGE	COST	NOTES

MEDICAL TREATMENT

NAME/ ID	DATE/ PERIOD	DX/ CONDITION	TREATMENT/TEST/ PROCEDURE	DOSAGE	COST	NOTES

MEDICAL TREATMENT

NAME/ ID	DATE/ PERIOD	DX/ CONDITION	TREATMENT/TEST/ PROCEDURE	DOSAGE	COST	NOTES

MEDICAL TREATMENT

NAME/ ID	DATE/ PERIOD	DX/ CONDITION	TREATMENT/TEST/ PROCEDURE	DOSAGE	COST	NOTES

MEDICAL TREATMENT

NAME/ ID	DATE/ PERIOD	DX/ CONDITION	TREATMENT/TEST/ PROCEDURE	DOSAGE	COST	NOTES

SUPPLEMENTATION RECORD

HERD/ ID	# OF ANIMALS	PERIOD	FEED TYPE/ COMBINATION	QTY	TOTAL LBS/WK	COST	NOTES

SUPPLEMENTATION RECORD

HERD/ ID	# OF ANIMALS	PERIOD	FEED TYPE/ COMBINATION	QTY	TOTAL LBS/WK	COST	NOTES

SUPPLEMENTATION RECORD

HERD/ ID	# OF ANIMALS	PERIOD	FEED TYPE/ COMBINATION	QTY	TOTAL LBS/WK	COST	NOTES

SUPPLEMENTATION RECORD

HERD/ ID	# OF ANIMALS	PERIOD	FEED TYPE/ COMBINATION	QTY	TOTAL LBS/WK	COST	NOTES

SUPPLEMENTATION RECORD

HERD/ ID	# OF ANIMALS	PERIOD	FEED TYPE/ COMBINATION	QTY	TOTAL LBS/WK	COST	NOTES

SUPPLEMENTATION RECORD

HERD/ ID	# OF ANIMALS	PERIOD	FEED TYPE/ COMBINATION	QTY	TOTAL LBS/WK	COST	NOTES

SUPPLEMENTATION RECORD

HERD/ ID	# OF ANIMALS	PERIOD	FEED TYPE/ COMBINATION	QTY	TOTAL LBS/WK	COST	NOTES

SUPPLEMENTATION RECORD

HERD/ ID	# OF ANIMALS	PERIOD	FEED TYPE/ COMBINATION	QTY	TOTAL LBS/WK	COST	NOTES

SUPPLEMENTATION RECORD

HERD/ ID	# OF ANIMALS	PERIOD	FEED TYPE/ COMBINATION	QTY	TOTAL LBS/WK	COST	NOTES

SUPPLEMENTATION RECORD

HERD/ ID	# OF ANIMALS	PERIOD	FEED TYPE/ COMBINATION	QTY	TOTAL LBS/WK	COST	NOTES

SUPPLEMENTATION RECORD

HERD/ ID	# OF ANIMALS	PERIOD	FEED TYPE/ COMBINATION	QTY	TOTAL LBS/WK	COST	NOTES

SUPPLEMENTATION RECORD

HERD/ ID	# OF ANIMALS	PERIOD	FEED TYPE/ COMBINATION	QTY	TOTAL LBS/WK	COST	NOTES

SUPPLEMENTATION RECORD

HERD/ ID	# OF ANIMALS	PERIOD	FEED TYPE/ COMBINATION	QTY	TOTAL LBS/WK	COST	NOTES

SUPPLEMENTATION RECORD

HERD/ ID	# OF ANIMALS	PERIOD	FEED TYPE/ COMBINATION	QTY	TOTAL LBS/WK	COST	NOTES

SUPPLEMENTATION RECORD

HERD/ ID	# OF ANIMALS	PERIOD	FEED TYPE/ COMBINATION	QTY	TOTAL LBS/WK	COST	NOTES

SUPPLEMENTATION RECORD

HERD/ ID	# OF ANIMALS	PERIOD	FEED TYPE/ COMBINATION	QTY	TOTAL LBS/WK	COST	NOTES

DRESS OUT RECORD

NAME/ID	AGE	SEX	PROCESSING DATE	LIVE WT	HANGING WT	PRICE	NOTES

DRESS OUT RECORD

NAME/ ID	AGE	SEX	PROCESSING DATE	LIVE WT	HANGING WT	PRICE	NOTES

DRESS OUT RECORD

NAME/ID	AGE	SEX	PROCESSING DATE	LIVE WT	HANGING WT	PRICE	NOTES

DRESS OUT RECORD

NAME/ ID	AGE	SEX	PROCESSING DATE	LIVE WT	HANGING WT	PRICE	NOTES

DRESS OUT RECORD

NAME/ ID	AGE	SEX	PROCESSING DATE	LIVE WT	HANGING WT	PRICE	NOTES

DRESS OUT RECORD

NAME/ ID	AGE	SEX	PROCESSING DATE	LIVE WT	HANGING WT	PRICE	NOTES

DRESS OUT RECORD

NAME/ ID	AGE	SEX	PROCESSING DATE	LIVE WT	HANGING WT	PRICE	NOTES

DRESS OUT RECORD

NAME/ ID	AGE	SEX	PROCESSING DATE	LIVE WT	HANGING WT	PRICE	NOTES

DRESS OUT RECORD

NAME/ ID	AGE	SEX	PROCESSING DATE	LIVE WT	HANGING WT	PRICE	NOTES

DRESS OUT RECORD

NAME/ID	AGE	SEX	PROCESSING DATE	LIVE WT	HANGING WT	PRICE	NOTES

DRESS OUT RECORD

NAME/ID	AGE	SEX	PROCESSING DATE	LIVE WT	HANGING WT	PRICE	NOTES

DRESS OUT RECORD

NAME/ ID	AGE	SEX	PROCESSING DATE	LIVE WT	HANGING WT	PRICE	NOTES

DRESS OUT RECORD

NAME/ID	AGE	SEX	PROCESSING DATE	LIVE WT	HANGING WT	PRICE	NOTES

DRESS OUT RECORD

NAME/ ID	AGE	SEX	PROCESSING DATE	LIVE WT	HANGING WT	PRICE	NOTES

DRESS OUT RECORD

NAME/ ID	AGE	SEX	PROCESSING DATE	LIVE WT	HANGING WT	PRICE	NOTES

DRESS OUT RECORD

NAME/ID	AGE	SEX	PROCESSING DATE	LIVE WT	HANGING WT	PRICE	NOTES

Made in the USA
Columbia, SC
11 July 2025